California King Snakes

Caring For Your Pet California King Snake

California King Snake breeding, where to buy, types, care, temperament, cost, health, handling, husbandry, diet, and much more included!

By Lolly Brown

Copyrights and Trademarks

Disclaimer and Legal Notice

Foreword

The California Kingsnake is one of the most popular pet reptiles because of its ease of care, attractive appearance and docile demeanor. They are generally called Kingsnakes because they also eat other snakes, as does the king cobra. California Kingsnake is a relatively small subspecies of the common kingsnake and they are found in a variety of habitats.

Although California Kingsnake are truly a great choice as pets, these animals doesn't come with a thin instruction manual, but fear not! In this book you'll be easily guided on understanding your California Kingsnake; their behaviors, their characteristics, how you should feed and care for them and a whole lot more.

Embark on a wonderful journey of sharing your life with California Kingsnake. Learn to maximize the great privilege of living with one and be able to share this unique and unforgettable experience just like many "royal" pet snake owners that came before you!

Table of Contents

Introduction

When people think of pets, the first ones that come to mind are the classic choices – cats, dogs, birds, hamsters, and other usual domesticated animals. However, the number of people who want something more exotic and peculiar than the garden-variety furry creature is steadily increasing, and thus booms the demand for reptilian pets that include snakes! Yes you read that right snakes! You are obviously interested in snakes or have already had previous experience in handling one before that's why you're reading this book – and that's great! Keep learning.

Snakes, by nature, exude a certain kind of mystery for which some people have a preference. They are also relatively low key and quiet, and at the same time there is elegance in them that other animals cannot hope to match. Of course, there is also the additional panache that owning a pet snake gives to its owner; seeing as snakes are oftentimes portrayed as villains in any and all media types, showing how one can be tamed indeed leads to a certain advance in status or, at the very least, some bragging rights.

Snakes are seen as either friends or foes; they are enchanting or disturbing, delightful or terrifying. Obviously, snakes really do have a dangerous side for they are natural predators, and anyone who cannot account for this or is unwilling to embrace this fact should drop any lingering idea of keeping one as a pet. Snakes need dedication and determination in their care, and a prospective owner must be willing to exert effort to read up and completely comprehend what it means to take care of a snake and whatever duties that may entail.

If this is your first time taking a snake as a pet, then the California Kingsnake is perfect for you. California Kingsnakes are well-mannered and well-tempered beings, and their docile temperament makes them rather popular as a pet choice. They also have a long lifespan, averaging at around 20 years, which means that those who choose to keep them must be prepared for a long-term commitment.

The California Kingsnakes are more than just a pet; it is an exotic, elegant and also an interesting companion much like dogs and cats. These snakes are quite easy to handle, plus they are also very great family pets (if you're that certain type of family), although they may not be ideal for very young children. If you are thinking about rescuing or purchasing a snake, there are many types of variations you can choose from.

Before you bring a California Kingsnake home, however, you should be a responsible snake owner and learn everything you can about this breed and how to care for it properly.

Fortunately, this ultimate guide will teach you on how to be the best California Kingsnake owner you can be! Inside this book, you will find tons of helpful information about different types of California Kingsnakes; how they live, how to deal with them and realize the great benefits of owning one!

This book includes information about creating the ideal habitat and diet for your snake as well as tips for breeding and showing them to your friends or online. You will also find in-depth health information for the breed including common health problems affecting it and the treatment options available.

The serpent world awaits! Get ready for a wild yet exotic adventure!

Glossary of Snake Terms

1.2.3. (Numbers with full stops) – The numbers are used to denote the number of a species, arranged according to sex, thus: male.female.unknown sex. In this case, one male, two females, and three of unknown sex.

Acclimation – Adjusting to a new environment or new conditions over a period of time.

Active range – The area of activity which can include hunting, seeking refuge, and finding a mate.

Ambient temperature – The overall temperature of the environment.

Amelanistic – Amel for short; without melanin, or without any black or brown coloration.

Anal Plate – A modified ventral scale that covers and protects the vent; sometimes a single plate, sometimes a divided plate.

Anerythristic – Anery for short; without any red coloration.

Aquatic – Lives in water.

Arboreal – Lives in trees.

Betadine – An antiseptic that can be used to clean wounds in reptiles.

Bilateral – Where stripes, spots or markings are present on both sides of an animal.

Biotic – The living components of an environment.

Brille – A transparent scale above the eyes of snakes that allows them to see but also serves to protect the eyes at the same time. Also called Spectacle, and Ocular Scale.

Brumation – The equivalent of mammalian hibernation among reptiles.

Cannibalistic – Where an animal feeds on others of its own kind.

Caudocephalic Waves – The ripple-like contractions that move from the rear to the front of a snake's body.

CB – Captive Bred, or bred in captivity.

CH – Captive Hatched.

Cloaca – also Vent; a half-moon shaped opening for digestive waste disposal and sexual organs.

Cloacal Gaping – Indication of sexual receptivity of the female.

Cloacal Gland – A gland at the base of the tail which emits foul smelling liquid as a defense mechanism; also called Anal Gland.

Clutch – A batch of eggs.

Constriction – The act of wrapping or coiling around a prey to subdue and kill it prior to eating.

Crepuscular – Active at twilight, usually from dusk to dawn.

Crypsis – Camouflage or concealing.

Diurnal – Active by day

Drop – To lay eggs or to bear live young.

Ectothermic – Cold-blooded. An animal that cannot regulate its own body temperature, but sources body heat from the surroundings.

Endemic – Indigenous to a specific region or area.

Estivation – Also Aestivation; a period of dormancy that usually occurs during the hot or dry seasons in order to escape the heat or to remain hydrated.

Faunarium (Faun) – A plastic enclosure with an air holed lid, usually used for small animals such as hatchling snakes, lizards, and insects.

FK – Fresh Killed; a term usually used when feeding a rodent that is recently killed, and therefore still warm, to a pet snake.

Flexarium – A reptile enclosure that is mostly made from mesh screening, for species that require plenty of ventilation.

Fossorial – A burrowing species.

Fuzzy – For rodent prey, one that has just reached the stage of development where fur is starting to grow.

F/T – Frozen/thawed; used to refer to food items that are frozen but thawed before feeding to your pet.

Gestation – The period of development of an embryo within a female.

Gravid – The equivalent of pregnant in reptiles.

Glottis – A tube-like structure that projects from the lower jaw of a snake to facilitate ingestion of large food items.

Gut-loading – Feeding insects within 24 hours to a prey before they are fed to your pet, so that they pass on the nutritional benefits.

Hatchling – A newly hatched, or baby, reptile.

Hemipenes – Dual sex organs; common among male snakes.

Hemipenis – A single protrusion of a paired sexual organ; one half is used during copulation.

Herps/Herpetiles – A collective name for reptile and amphibian species.

Herpetoculturist – A person who keeps and breeds reptiles in captivity.

Herpetologist – A person who studies ectothermic animals, sometimes also used for those who keeps reptiles.

Herpetology – The study of reptiles and amphibians.

Hide Box – A furnishing within a reptile cage that gives the animal a secure place to hide.

Hots – Venomous.

Husbandry – The daily care of a pet reptile.

Hygrometer – Used to measure humidity.

Impaction – A blockage in the digestive tract due to the swallowing of an object that cannot be digested or broken down.

Incubate – Maintaining eggs in conditions favorable for development and hatching.

Interstitial – The skin between scales.

Intromission – Also mating; when the male's hemipenis is inserted into the cloaca of the female.

Juvenile – Not yet adult; not of breedable age.

LTC – Long Term Captive; or one that has been in captivity for more than six months.

MBD – Metabolic Bone Disease; occurs when reptiles lack sufficient calcium in their diet.

Morph – Color pattern

Musking – Secretion of a foul smelling liquid from its vent as a defense mechanism.

Oviparous – Egg-bearing.

Ovoviviparous – Eggs are retained inside the female's body until they hatch.

Pinkie – Newborn rodent.

Pip – The act of a hatchling snake to cut its way out of the egg using a special egg tooth.

PK – Pre-killed; a term used when live rodents are not fed to a snake.

Popping – The process by which the sex is determined among hatchlings.

Probing – The process by which the sex is determined among adults.

Regurgitation – Also Regurge; occurs when a snake regurgitates or brings out a half-digested meal.

R.I. – Respiratory Infection; common condition among reptiles kept in poor conditions.

Serpentine Locomotion – The manner in which snakes move.

Sloughing – Shedding.

Sub-adult – Juvenile.

Substrate – The material lining the bottom of a reptile enclosure.

Stat – Short for Thermostat

Tag – Slang for a bite or being bitten

Terrarium – A reptile enclosure.

Thermo-regulation – The process by which cold-blooded animals regulate their body temperature by moving from hot to cold surroundings.

Vent – Cloaca

Vivarium – Glass-fronted enclosure

Viviparous – Gives birth to live young.

WC – Wild Caught.

Weaner – A sub-adult rodent.

WF – Wild Farmed; refers to the collection of a pregnant female whose eggs or young were hatched or born in captivity.

Yearling – A year old.

Zoonosis – A disease that can be passed from animal to man.

Chapter One: California Kingsnake in Focus

California Kingsnake is a great twist in a traditional pet, but before you bring home your slithery new side kick, be sure that you are ready and that you know how you can handle it, otherwise, they will handle you. (Trust me, you don't want that). Bringing home a snake can be an exciting and fun event for both you and your new pet. With a little prep ahead of time, your snake can be tamed and be socialized with the right handling.

California Kingsnakes are very popular pets not only because they are very easy to care for and have great personalities, but also because they are very available in a seemingly endless variety of different morphs. They are very docile and beautiful. They average about 3 to 4 feet and come in a variety of patterns and colors. They are not too big and they usually have a good temperament.

Kingsnakes belong to the members of the family Colubridae and the subfamily Colubrinae. Colubrid snakes are from the large family of nonvenomous snakes that can be found around the world such as North America. Kingsnakes are members of the genus *Lampropeltis,* which means "shiny shields" in Greek. This genus is known for its well-defined, glossy scales.

Adult king snakes should be kept in at least 20 galloon enclosures, but if they are still babies, they can be perfectly content in a shoe box. Kingsnakes are escape artists so it is highly recommended that it has a secure lid. You may not want to let these serpent Houdinis escape and wander around the house without you knowing.

California Kingsnake can get up to 5 to 7 feet and they will live anywhere from 10 to 25 years, so be ready to enjoy it for a long time when you start with.

These types of snake are very aggressive and skilled hunters. They usually eat rodents, lizards, birds and bird eggs. They are called Kingsnakes because sometimes, they eat other snakes, like the King Cobra. In fact, this nonvenomous snake can even devour and kill highly venomous snakes.

California Kingsnakes can make a novel and interesting pet. It is widely regarded as one of the best snakes to keep as a pet. And if you happen to want to have one, be sure to choose one bred legally in captivity, not one captured illegally in the wild. This snake is good natured, gentle and can respond well to interactions with humans.

The size of a California Kingsnake ranges from 27 cm to 76 cm. Its color may come in dark brown or black with whitish-yellow bands. They have vibrant patterns on their skin with vivid contrasting colors. Their bands and speckles break up the snake's body outline so their visibility to the predators is less visible.

California Kingsnake can be your best friend. People love them for their beauty while rattlesnakes fear them because of their dominance. Some people sleep and eat with them which just show that California Kingsnakes are indeed a great companion. They can definitely meet your basic psychological needs in pretty much the way humans do.

They can make you feel socially content, with the result of feeling better about life in general. Isn't that awesome?

The California Kingsnakes are very interesting in both personality and aesthetics and can really be a great pet but it is recommended that you research first before getting one because owning one is not something that you can just assume or overlooked.

The next section will give you an overview of the California Kingsnakes and some of its interesting facts. It will also guide you on the decision of owning one as having this type of pet is something different – it is royalty!

Facts about California Kingsnake

California Kingsnakes are admired by many because of its unique personality and beautiful appearance. These snakes have a variety of morphs and can be even found in albino. California Kingsnakes come in black, brown, or dark blue/purplish bands that form a pattern with yellow or white bands running down the entire snake's body.

Generally, California Kingsnakes have smooth, shiny scales that can be ringed, striped, spotted or a combination.

These stripes can go across the body or stripes going down the body from the head to the tail. It is found in wide variety of habitats woodlands, forests, grasslands, chaparrals, farmlands, deserts, marshes, and even suburban areas. Mostly, they are terrestrial but they may climb low branches and shrubs.

The California Kingsnake is diurnal, which means they are active in daytime but when it is hot they can often become nocturnal, or being active at night. When disturbed or threatened, they can give off a strong musk odor. Its tail will vibrate quickly, hiss, and roll into a ball, hiding its head in a defense posture.

When subduing their prey, they usually use constriction and they are also capable of swallowing a whole rattlesnake while it is still alive. They also have a tolerance to rattlesnake's venom.

California Kingsnakes are considered the "king" of the snakes because of their great ability in preying other snakes. They are not too big, as mentioned earlier, they are averaging about 3 to 4 feet and they usually have a good temperament.

Humans benefit from them because of their role in the ecosystem, controlling rodent, and frog populations and killing rattlesnakes.

It's very important to research first all the information about California Kingsnake before deciding to own one. It's something that you have to do. The first thing that you need to consider about snakes is they are not dogs or cats or fish or birds or guinea pig or any other animal. They are something different. They are snakes. A snake is an animal that has to be respected. You can't just train it to behave the way that you want it to behave. You have to respect its behavior. If it doesn't like to be handled then don't handle it. If it bites you, you can't punish it.

It's also very important to figure out the reason why you want it. If you just want a snake because it looks cool and it's really badass and it's like an awesome fashion statement, don't do it. Just go buy necklace or a pair of shoes or something. A snake is a living animal. It's not some just an accessory. You have to care for it, and love it and nurture it and look after it and everything else. They are a living creature and you can't just buy one just because you have an epic vision of you lying in your bed being in all sexy with your pet snake.

Next thing you should need to figure out is the age you want to buy. Baby snakes are referred to as hatchlings. The younger that you start handling a snake generally the better temperament they will have for the rest of their lives.

You should also consider their feeding habit, where to buy a reputable one, and also their shedding routines and schedule. There's obviously a lot more about owning a California Kingsnake, so keep reading!

Quick Facts

Scientific Name: *Lampropeltis getula californiae*

Size as they hatch from their eggs: 8 to 12 inches.

Maximum adult size: 6 feet in length

Average size: 3 to 4 feet

Birth Date: Unknown

Wild Diet: Feeds largely but not exclusively on other snakes. They also eat birds, rodents, lizards and have the ability to consume rattlesnakes with no apparent ill effect

Museum Diet: Mice and small rats.

Life Span in the Wild: 10 to 15 years

Life Span in Captivity: 15 to 20 years

Habitat: varied, can be found in pine forests or in rocky outcrops, brushy semi-desert areas, and brushy hillsides.

Distribution and Range: Baja California, east to western Arizona and north to Oregon and Southern Utah.

Chapter Two: California Kingsnake Requirements

Are you now thinking of getting a California Kingsnake as a pet? Really? Wow, you're weird – weirdly elegant! After knowing what they are, their characteristics, and how to deal with them, it's time to give you practical tips on what you need to know before buying one.

In this chapter, you will get a whole lot of information on its pros and cons, its average associated costs as well as the legal licensing you need so that you will be well on your way to becoming a legitimate California Kingsnake pet owner – should you decide to be one! Let's do this!

First of all, you should ask yourself exactly why you want to keep a California Kingsnake as a pet. California Kingsnake has an average lifespan of 20 years! It's like raising a child. But if you are only considering getting a California Kingsnake as a status symbol, then you should rethink your choices. As much as California Kingsnake would make a wonderful addition to your household with their natural elegance and exquisiteness, their care would also demand much of your commitment. The responsibilities you would have to carry include feeding them, cleaning after them, seeing to their maintenance, and understanding their behavior.

California Kingsnake can be quite aggressive creatures, and their defense mechanism involves a lot of eating, even their own kind, however California Kingsnake also responds fairly well to human touch especially if it is constant, so you would have to make sure that you do not neglect them. They are not picky eaters but it can definitely eat you alive, so please watch out. You will also have to check them constantly for ticks and mites and their overall health.

Simply put, California Kingsnake requires a fair amount of guarantee that you will be there to take care of them and make sure they are okay. You cannot take care of a California Kingsnake halfway, and you have to be all in –

starting with recognizing within yourself if you have what it takes to take care of this lovely and royal creature.

License Requirements

California Kingsnakes can be kept as pets as long as you have a license. Like any other pets, native reptiles are protected by law so if you want to keep one as a pet, you'll need a license from the Office of Environment and Heritage (National Perks and Wildlife Service)

California Kingsnakes must be bought from licensed dealers or breeders. Licensing is important because it will protect your Kingsnakes species and their ecosystems. It also keeps the reptiles and their owners safe. Also, licensing helps people/pet owners abide by NSW laws.

There are different types of license depending on the number of animals you own and how difficult they are to keep. It is required that you demonstrate your experience and training if you are planning to keep venomous reptiles, like Kingsnakes.

As a reminder there is no federal law governing private possession or ownership of exotic animals in the United States. You need to pay attention not on a national level but on a local level, with your local and state laws and ordinances, to see what is permitted and what is not.

The regulations vary from one city/state to another, as some outright ban or prohibit exotic or dangerous animals, while others simply call for permits that set down requirements such as micro-chipping, an established relationship with a veterinarian, and even insurance. Some may also ask you to present proof that you are acquiring the animal from a recognized breeder and that the snake was bred in captivity (as opposed to being captured from the wild), so acquiring a license from the Office of Environment and Heritage can really help.

It is also a good idea to check the rules about keeping pet snakes based on where you are - city, town, neighborhood, and even in the apartment building, if applicable. All these are reasonable precautions to take simply for the fact that should you ever be found to be keeping such a pet illegally, the discovery could result in consequences such as fines or, worse, the confiscation of your pet. You might not even be able to find a veterinarian willing to give your California Kingsnake medical care if you are found to be keeping it without the correct permits.

Permits may also be necessary for importing, exporting, or traveling with an exotic or a naturally dangerous animal.

You also need to be constantly updated on information regarding your local state laws at least once every six months. Regulations can change, and you don't want to find yourself suddenly in violation of a law which was amended after you thought you had abided by it a year ago.

If all this seems complicated and really overwhelming, you have to remind yourself that you are bringing a potentially dangerous animal into a human community. One that can definitely eat your neighbor alive! As such, restrictions and limitations should be expected so that the safety of anyone involved will be ensured.

It must also be noted as a point of fact that the illegal trade in exotic animals has been an immensely profitable business for backyard breeders and illegal importers. If you care about these animals at all, you shouldn't support activities which promote their unlawful capture from the wild or the breeding and transport of these animals in inappropriate and pitiless conditions.

How Many California Kingsnake Should You Keep?

California Kingsnake, being one of the most well-mannered python types, may not be an ideal choice for first-time snake-keepers. They can adapt well with regular human contact but they need an owner who can handle them with care. Their quite aggressive nature is not suitable for families with young children.

Just like when considering other pets, the decision of whether you can keep more than one California Kingsnake or not depends on your overall capacity to commit to all of them. The only risk is that since this snake is quite a dominant type, it might end up eating another breed of snake to show them who is the King. It's probably better to separate them from one another to avoid competition.

Of course, you must also keep in mind that keeping more than one California Kingsnake means an increase in responsibility financially, timewise, and even mentally.

Efforts of cleanup and cage maintenance will be doubled, or tripled, and can definitely take up all your time. Before committing to it, you should assess your capacity (financially, mentally and timely) to provide what your pets will require without fail. You will have to be completely ready and prepared because you're about to serve a King!

Taking care of one California Kingsnake is already a lot, especially if this is your first time owning a snake as a pet. Be sure to make an informed and responsible decision on how many California Kingsnake you can responsibly and dutifully care for and keep.

California Kingsnake with Other Pets

The California Kingsnake is a carnivorous natural predator, and when in the wild, they kill their prey by constricting it and swallowing even the most venomous and dangerous snakes (they're a King remember?). Adult California Kingsnake are also known to feed on adult mice, rats, or young chickens, because of this, California Kingsnake they can pose real threat to your dog, cat, child or even you! If they feel threatened at all, they will kill you.

As stated before, California Kingsnake can be quite aggressive if not handled or trained properly. They can be a recommended snake to have if you are looking for a more challenging pet or if you're already an expert in taking care of snakes.

Ease and Cost of Care

Before acquiring a California Kingsnake, you have to give some thought to how much it will really cost. You really have to invest and commit on their expenses if you genuinely want to own one so that you can maintain their healthy lifestyle and environment properly.

The initial purchase price is only one very small part of the overall cost of a California Kingsnake. Just like any other pet snakes, the Kingsnake requires vet visits, food, shelter, water, and more. Unlike dogs and cats, snakes require especially suited place to live in. Heating pads and lights running 24/7 will rise up your energy bills very quickly.

Purchase Price: $30 - $100 or more

So how much would it take to purchase a King? You'd be surprise! California Kingsnake usually range anywhere from $30 to $40 from breeders. Pet stores charge double the price, often $100 or more. It is much better to find a breeder so you can save a lot. If you only ever buy one snake this will be the only time you'll need to count this cost in your figures.

Glass Aquarium: average of $100

This will be the main habitat of your snake, if I were you, I'd really buy something that is of great quality. Don't forget that you're keeping a Kingsnake, they can easily break the glass or escape the aquarium (they're the Houdinis of the serpent world remember?) so it's better to purchase a really thick glass that can also be a comfortable resting place for your pet.

Under Tank Heater (UTH): $25 to $30

The under tank heater is needed to control the temperature inside the aquarium for your snake. Usually costs about $25 to $30 or more depending on the brand or quality. Tanks need to be changed as your snake grows which means that you need to replace them and buy more tanks in the future.

Heat Lamp Setup: ranges from $50 to $75

Just like the UTH, this serves as a heater for your snake. You might want to save up for this because it is quite costly it can range from $50 - $75. Bulbs can burn out which means that you need to buy every now and then.

Substrate: $15 to $25

You can buy a bag that will last about 4 to 6 weeks, it can cost anywhere from $15 to $25. It also depends on the brand or quality.

Caging Materials: $25 to $50

This includes a hiding space, water bowls, climbing branches, fake foliage, and other materials inside the cage that will stimulate your snake and can simulate its natural habitat. This will have a total estimate cost of $25 to $50.

Food: $50 to $200

You need to feed your California Kingsnake mice, rats or live chickens, with a particular amount (see feeding guide section). It will cost about $50 to as high as $200 in a month.

Veterinary: $100 - $125

In order to keep your California Kingsnake healthy you should take him to the veterinarian at least every year or twice a year. Since snakes are a specialized animal you'll likely pay more than you would for a cat or a dog. The average cost for an annual vet visit for a snake is about $100

\- $125 or more not to mention the other medical costs that may come up if your pet gets sick.

Emergency Costs of keeping a California Kingsnake

Let's assume that your snake bites someone or some other people's pet. Are you prepared to pay for their medical bills and lawyer fees if it is necessary? Will you be able to afford the expenses to take care of it? This can happen and you should be financially well-off to handle it.

Overview of Expenses

Needs	Costs
Purchase Price	$30 - $100 (£24.06 - £80.21)
Glass Aquarium	$100 (£80.21)
Under Tank Heater	$25 - $30 (£20.05 - £24.06)
Heat Lamp	$50 - $75 (£40.11 - £60.16)
Substrate	$15 - $25 (£12.03 - £20.05)
Caging Materials	$25 - $50

	(£20.05 - £40.11)
Food	$50 - $200
	(£40.11 - £160.42)
Veterinary Care	$100 - $125
	(£80.21 - £100.26)
Total	$395 - $705
	(£316.84 - £565.49)

*Costs may vary depending on location
**Costs may change based on the currency exchange

Pros and Cons of California Kingsnakes

Before you bring a California Kingsnake home you should take the time to learn the pros and cons of the breed. Every snake breed is different so you need to think about the details to determine whether a California Kingsnake is actually the right pet for you.

In this section you will find a list of pros and cons for California Kingsnake:

Pros

- California Kingsnakes come in a wide variety of colors

- California Kingsnakes are easy to take care and challenging at the same time

- California Kingsnakes are relatively inexpensive to feed.

- California Kingsnakes are readily available in most pet stores.

- Unlike hamsters and other rodents, California Kingsnakes do not smell
- California Kingsnakes live for a very long time compared to most pets, so you do not have to worry about them passing away as often as dogs or cats, and you definitely don't need to replace them as often as you'd need to replace a hamster.

- California Kingsnakes, as being exotic pets, are more rarely owned than dogs, cats, and rodents. This makes them more appealing than having a more common pet; having a pet snake is cool.

Cons

- Unlike other reptiles, California Kingsnakes do not eat worms, insects, or baby food; they eat rats (and sometimes mice, though rats are much healthier for them)

- It might be hard to find someone who will feed your Kingsnake for you if ever you are gone or on vacation. They are snakes after all and there may not be many people who would like feeding a rat to them.

- It may be difficult to find a veterinarian who can take care of your Kingsnake if it's ill. Before you buy them, you should look around first and find out where the closest California Kingsnake vet is located.

- Certain California Kingsnakes morphs are overpriced by particular dealers.

Chapter Three: Purchasing Your California Kingsnake

Now that you are already aware and have prior knowledge about the legal aspects of owning and maintaining a California Kingsnake as well as its pros and cons, the next step is purchasing one through a local farm pet store or a legitimate breeder. In this chapter you will find valuable information about where to find a California Kingsnake breeder, how to select a reputable breeder, and the questions you need to ask from your potential supplier. You will also receive tips for your home and for introducing your new pet snake to your family.

This chapter will give you some basic tips in looking for the best Kingsnake breeder. It is very important to find a suitable breeder in the market that fits you. By then, you must be prepared in providing adequate care for whichever one you end up buying.

Finding a Reputable Kingsnake Breeder

It is indeed important that your California Kingsnake should come from a reputable local breeder. These breeders must be knowledgeable about the breeds they raise and they have to know about the relevant genetics. They have to take note that the primary reason for breeding a snake is for health and appearance comes in secondary only. Some breeders are very much concerned about appearance, of course, including colors and markings, but the most beautiful California Kingsnake is no good if it's not healthy.

It is preferred to deal with small breeders because they're more knowledgeable about the Kingsnakes they're selling and producing. They can teach you the complete set-ups and inform you about your species' temperaments, preferred cages and other details you need to know. Breeders tend to know a lot about the species they breed, so they often can supply more information than a typical pet store clerk, according to Byron J. S. de la Navarre, DVM, a Chicago-based past president of the Association of Reptilian and Amphibian Veterinarians (ARAV).

You can make a list of the breeders who specialize in California Kingsnakes. This is becoming easier to do with the help of the internet. A bit of Google search magic can help you find these people. Other places to look for breeders are the Kingsnake breeder directory and the fauna classifieds websites. Also, you can look for online communities that specialize in Kingsnakes and you'll often find that those forums have a place for people to list either businesses or individual snakes for sale. Also, the website pet-snakes.com has a list of breeders in our snakes by state section.

If you are still having some problems in finding a breeder, you may want to try contacting another breeder and asking them if they can recommend anyone to you. The reptile community group is a tight knit group and it's very common for people to recommend one another even if competition exists between the parties.

Next thing to do after making a list is contacting the breeders and start talking specifics. Get a feel for what they know about their Kingsnakes. There are some places that appear to be breeder but they are not. They may work directly with importers who provide them the animals instead of producing them in their own. There is a great chance that they might not have any information about the Kingsnakes that they are selling.

Be sure not to waste their times because they have business to run just like anyone else. It is recommended to ask relevant questions about their breeding practices. This is a relevant exercise for a few reasons:

- **It will tell you who you are doing business with**

A good breeder who is passionate about the animals that they breed will want to talk to you about them. They will not hesitate to answer your questions and at the same time ask questions of their own. If a breeder doesn't bother to answer all of your questions in order to get you to spend money with them do you think they will be responsive after the sale?

- **It establishes a relationship between yourself and the breeder:**

If you're going to spend hundreds of dollars with someone who you only know online, wouldn't you like them to know as much about you in regards to the snakes you will buy from them as possible? It sure does, and almost everyone else does as well. That is why it is very important to establish a relationship with the breeder.

- **Sometimes you'll find a better deal:**

You must not be limited to Kingsnakes listed on a breeders' website. You may need to ask the breeder if they had any other Kingsnakes other than what was listed.

Those three reasons alone are sure enough to convince you that opening a dialogue between you and the snake breeder is not only a good idea, but a prudent one too.

In choosing the right breeder, you must pick the one you are most comfortable with. Your decision on which breeders you will be most comfortable buying a Kingsnake from must be based on your research and communications. You may have a list of three or four. One is going to be the primary and the others will be "just in case". At this point, you may ask for references and sometimes, it may be good to wait. Why? Because one might be selling what they have bred for the first time and has no references at that point although they are a really good and honorable person.

Ask the reference at least three to five questions about anything you want to know about their Kingsnake. You can ask whatever questions related to the purchase of the snake. The following are some guides in asking questions to the reference:

- How many Kingsnakes have you bought from [breeder name]?

- Have you ever had any issues with DOA specimens?

- After the sale how has the communication been?

- Would you buy another snake from them right now?

- Can you provide me the contact information of anyone else you know who has bought from this snake breeder in the past?

Those are just some examples you may want to ask a reference. Bottom line is the purpose of asking questions is to make your decision easier.

At some point you'll need to decide who you will be

buying your Kingsnake from. Once you've made a research on the species of snake you are interested in buying; made a list of breeders who sell California Kingsnakes; contacted the breeders in your list; choose the breeder you are most comfortable with and finally speak to the references, then you are ready to make a purchase. Once all of the leg-work is done, purchasing the snake is the easy part, simply because you are already well-informed.

Buying a snake can be daunting, but when you find a good breeder, they will walk you through every step of the process. They are willing to answer all of your questions and if they think that you are not a good fit as an owner, they won't sell it to you. Yes, they want to earn money but they also want to protect the integrity of the hobby. That's usually a great sign that the breeder really care about the pets.

Questions to Ask From a Snake Breeder

Owners who buy straight from a breeder can likely expect to pay higher than buying from a pet store, but not always. Unlike pet shops, a breeder does not have to deal with costs of paying employees and leasing a space that leads to higher markups on animals for sale. Other breeders will also choose to sell their breeds in a cheaper price than expected to undercut their competition.

You can ask questions in order to screen breeders under consideration. Some of these questions may include:

- How many years have you been in business, and what kind of experience do you have as a breeder?

- What do you specialize in? What types of species do you breed and sell?

- Do you offer any kind of a warranty or guarantee?

- Who are your customers?

- Have you received any complaints or negative feedback online or from the Better Business Bureau?

- Can you provide the names and numbers of at least three recent private individuals you have sold to, who I can contact to gauge their satisfaction in buying from you?

Choosing a California Kingsnake

After you have narrowed down your list of options to just two or three snake breeders, your next step is to actually pick out the snake you want. You have already determined that the remaining breeders on your list are responsible, but now you need to make sure that the California Snake they have available are healthy and ready to go home with their new owners.

You should choose a Kinsgsnake that look healthy, with a bright eyes and good skin condition. It must not be too fat or too thin. Purchase your Kingsnake from a reputable breeder. Determining the sex of a snake can be challenging so you need a vet or an expert that will help to tell you. It is not recommended to own a snake if you have young children in the house or someone who has a poor immune system since snakes carry a small risk of salmonella.

- **Examine the Snake's Body**
  Examine the snakes body for signs of any illness and potential injury.
- **Eyes:** The snake should have clear, bright eyes with no discharge.
- **Body:** The snake's body must be lean and the length should be appropriate for its age.

- **Mobility:** The snake should be able to swiftly move normally without any mobility problems.

List of Snake Breeders

Here is the list of breeders and adoption rescue websites around United States and United Kingdom:

United States Kingsnake Breeders

Back Water Reptiles
<http://www.backwaterreptiles.com/kingsnakes/california-king-snake-for-sale.html>

Snakes at Sunset
<http://snakesatsunset.com/desert-striped-california-king-snake-for-sale-lampropeltis-getula/>

BHB Reptiles
<https://www.bhbreptiles.com/collections/king-snakes>

Reptiles by Mack
<http://www.reptilesbymack.com/king-snakes.aspx>

Liz King Snakes

<http://www.lizskingsnakes.com/>

Underground Reptiles

<https://undergroundreptiles.com/product-category/animals/snakes/kingsnakes/>

VM Sherp

<http://www.vmsherp.com/ViewKingsnakes.htm>

<u>United Kingdom Snake Breeders</u>

PreLoved UK

<http://www.preloved.co.uk/classifieds/pets/reptiles/for-sale/uk/california+king+snake>

Pets4Homes UK

<https://www.pets4homes.co.uk/sale/reptiles/king-snake/>

Reptile Trader

<http://www.reptiletrader.co.uk/exotic-pets/119>

Chapter Four: Maintenance for California Kingsnake

Having a pet snake is something different and sometimes, maintenance can be a struggle. It truly comes with a great deal of responsibility. If you happen to decide to buy your own California Kingsnake, you have to be sure that you can provide their necessities so that it will stay healthy and happy. This chapter will give you basic information in maintaining a California Kingsnake including tips on setting up their enclosure, a complete guide in taking care of them and ways on how to keep your Kingsnakes happy.

Tips on How to Set-up your Kingsnake's Terrarium

Heating

Reptiles are cold-blooded so they can't produce their own body heat. In setting up a Kingsnake's enclosure, be sure to have heating to warm up their blood and keep all their organs moving. There are a few options that you can go for with heating. There are heat mats, there are heat lamps which basically mimicks the sun and then there are heat strips which are generally used with snake rack system. A lot of breeders will use stripping and it works pretty much the same as the heat mat.

A heat mat is stuck to the bottom of the outside of your enclosure and it will just heat up the floor. Never consider buying a heat rock as a source of heat. They are so unpredictable and they are very renowned for causing burns on animals because they can't regulate the temperature of heat rock properly.

Water

The second thing you need in your tank is water. It seems really obvious but it must be iterated that snakes need water to live.

Hide

The third thing that you need is what's referred to as hide. It is quite literally use for your snake to hide. In nature, that's what snakes do. They hide and then they go out in the sun for a little bit, they warm up and then go back in and they'll hide again. There are a lot of pre-made hides available that you can get from pretty much any pet store.

It may be a log or a rock but you can just make anything just like having that a box with a hole in it. It is not recommended to get anything super fancy or expensive while your snake is still growing because as it grows you're going to need a new hide. So until it's fully grown don't bother getting anything too extraordinary because you're just going to need to replace it soon anyway.

Substrate

The fourth thing that you need is a substrate. Substrate is the stuff that you put on the bottom of your tank. A lot of people will just use newspapers or paper towels because it's cost effective. It does look a bit unappealing but it's not bad for a snake. If you like you can find out what Kingsnakes have naturally in their environment in the wild. You can naturally use that but honestly your snake is really going to know the difference.

Other than that, what you put in your tank is optionally up to you. You can decorate it however you want or you could just leave really plain.

Caring Tips for Your California Kingsnake

- Put your snakes alone in its terrarium or with appropriate buddies.

- Feed your snakes alone to avoid food aggression.

- Feed your Kingsnake mice. Freshly killed mice are the best choice. One mouse per week will be enough, but if you want your Kingsnake to grow faster, you can give it up to two per week.

- Be sure to stay away from your snake until the lump from the mouse disappears. Don't carry your snake up until it has digested the mouse enough that the lump in its middle has disappeared, because it might still feel aggressive before its food is digested

- Provide fresh water. Use a relatively deep bowl, check the water bowl every day and always keep it clean. If the Kingsnake starts to feel very moist, take the water bowl out and return it for a few days every week.

- Handle your snake gently. Keep in mind that this is a wild animal, so it may be afraid of you for quite some time. Gently hold your snake and stay away from its face, especially at first.

- Watch for shedding. Never handle your snake when you think it's getting ready to shed. It will be obvious that this is happening when their skin starts to turn milky or bluish. In just a few days, they'll crawl completely out of their old skin, and by then, it will be safe to hold them again.

- Don't restrain your snake. California king snakes almost never bite, but if you restrain them, they may. Never pinch or squeeze them. Let them flow gently through your hands and fingers.

Keeping an Eye Out for Common Problems

- Find a vet who is expert about snakes. You may have to travel to find a competent vet since most vets don't come in contact with snakes that often that is why it is a great idea to get connected with one before anything goes wrong.

- Watch for mites. Mites love to live on king snakes. Keep an eye out especially around their mouth, eyes, and under their scales. If ever your snake becomes lethargic or not eating, this might be caused by mites so always give them an inspection.

- Keep an eye out for respiratory infections. If your Kingsnake sounds wheezy or experience excessive saliva, it may have a respiratory infection that may be caused by a dirty cage, low temperatures, or contact with another infected snake. In some cases, Kingsnakes will need an antibiotic so it's better to consult your vets.

- Pay attention to regurgitation. It's not unusual for Kingsnakes to regurgitate after eating but since this may be a sign of serious illness, you should keep an eye on your Kingsnake for other symptoms if you see them do this. If it happens most of the times, and your snake starts to lose weight, do not hesitate to take it to the vet.

Ways to Keep your California Kingsnake Happy

- Make sure your snake's vivarium is of a suitable size
- Correct vivarium temperature
- Maintain scrupulous hygiene

- Provide environmental enrichment
- Handle your California Kingsnake regularly & carefully
- Avoid stressing them out

Maintaining Humidity

A California Kingsnake enclosure should be kept at 50 percent humidity. If the humidity is extremely low, a daily misting will provide the higher humidity that aids in proper shedding. California Kingsnake should not be kept in a damp environment since this can lead to skin infections and other problems in your pet.

Useful Tools and Devices

As long as the basic requirement for a proper habitat is met, taking care of your California Kingsnake will get relatively easier. The trickiest part would be keeping the temperature and humidity at their proper levels, but once that's done, you won't have to think too much about other details. Fortunately enough, there are a number of devices and gadgets that can help you monitor these pertinent environmental factors. Using these, you can make sure that your California Kingsnake's habitat is the closest it can be to its natural requirements. A mistake in any of these – light, heat, or humidity – can cause various problems in your pet such as illnesses or diseases, behavioral changes, and sometimes even death – such as if temperature rises too high and causes them to dry out.

Some of the tools or gadgets you should perhaps invest in and familiarize yourself with include:

- A simple light timer to automate the on/off cycles of your light sources
- A thermometer to help you measure the heat and temperature
- A thermostat to help you in regulating the temperature by turning heating sources on and off as needed
- A rheostat can act as a dimmer, reducing or increasing the amount of power that goes to a certain device such as a light or heat source
- A hygrometer to help you monitor the humidity levels

Chapter Five: Nutritional Needs of California Kingsnake

While feeding your California Kingsnake might seem strange and difficult, it is actually fairly simple. You have to take in mind that snakes are predators and meat-eaters, so you have to see how comfortable you are with feeding animals to your snake before actually getting one as a pet. California Kingsnakes cover a broad spectrum of dietary requirements and it is very important to note that they maintain some degree of carnivore throughout their lifecycle.

They should be consuming appropriate-sized prey for proper nutrition. That is the basic fact that you need to know in owning a California Kingsnake. If you want a healthy snake, you should strive hard to give its proper nutrition and keep it that way.

This section will illustrate and explain how to properly feed your Kingsnake and their nutritional needs that they need to meet in order to maintain a healthy lifestyle.

Feeding California Kingsnakes

Generally, healthy captive – bred hatchlings generally feed consistently on frozen pinkie mice that were left out at room temperature or were thawed in warm water. You may over food to these hatchlings every five to seven days.

Sometimes, because of their given large environment, hatchling snakes feel insecure and may not eat. They often prefer feeding them if they are offered food in a small lidded deli cup with air holes in it. You can just leave them in the dark, undisturbed. The deli cup where the young snake is enclosed together with the pinkie mouse can be placed back into the tank during this time. After about a week, a young snake should adjust to its enclosure and can be able to adapt already to a more interactive feeding approach.

As your Kingsnake grows, there will be a wide variety of food items that you can feed him including fuzzy mice, hoppers, weanlings and, finally adult mice. A good rule of thumb of when feeding your Kingsnakes is to offer them prey no bigger than the widest part of the snake. Well, yes, California Kingsnakes can ingest prey much larger in girth than themselves, but, it is easier for the Kingsnake's digestive system to eat two smaller foods than choosing much larger ones.

If you observed that your Kingsnake stops eating thawed mice, they may be simply reverting them turning back to their older feeding habits. This can happen with both wild-caught juveniles and captive-bred snakes that were used to eat live meals for a long time as hatchlings. Breeders often use a couple of tricks to help urge the feeding response of stubborn snakes. Small lizards or anoles can be rubbed on live or thawed mice so they can smell them. Small number of a lizard's shed skin may also be put on the head of an offered pinkie. "Braining," is a technique often used when a pinkie mouse's head is split open. This may not sound good, but brained pinkies are very appetizing to baby snakes. If these techniques were used but your snake continues to refuse food, it may be an indication of a serious problem, where a veterinarian should be consulted.

California Kingsnake Food

In the wild, Kingsnakes will eat any bird or animal small enough to be swallowed whole. These include rattlesnakes. While in captivity, they should be fed rodents, usually mice which are easy to get because of its availability. You can offer live or well-thawed frozen mice to them but you should think twice of feeding them live adult mice because they can inflict wounds to your Kingsnakes. Fresh killed mice are the best choice.

Although California Kingsnakes prefer to eat rodents such as mice, especially in captivity, there are also a wide variety of choices which you can feed them. These are the following food choices, including those that they eat in the wild:

Small Rodents

Other rodents, besides rats, are what usually Kingsnakes eat. For example, mice are often fed to pet snakes because besides being an inexpensive food source, it is also nutritious for your Kingsnakes. If you are not comfortable with the idea of feeing your Kingsnakes live mice, you can feed them frozen mice that have thawed.

Eggs

Kingsnakes are well-known for eating chicken eggs. Besides the fact that eggs are easily sneaked from a bird's nest, it is also a good source of protein for your snake.

Small Birds and Fish

In the wild, Kingsnakes do not need to worry about chasing a bird away from its nest. Kingsnakes are large enough to ingest a small bird then it will eventually kill the parents and then eat the eggs. Baby birds are an easy meal for Kingsnakes. They also eat a variety of fish, ranging from small minnows up to large bass.

Snakes and Lizards

As mentioned earlier, Kingsnakes feed on other snakes and they are perhaps most famous for that habit. They are also known to eat lizards.

Frogs

Kingsnakes eat frogs but keep in mind that feeding frogs to Kingsnakes in captive puts it at risk.

Small Mmammals

California Kingsnakes have the venom or muscles to take down small mammals like foxes and coyotes.

Promoting Proper Eating Habits for Kingsnakes

The first thing you need to consider to make sure that your Kingsnake eats properly is to maintain and set up its habitat correctly. Kingsnakes have its own unique habitat requirements referring to lighting, temperature, humidity, layout, accessories, size of the habitat, and more. A Kingsnake that is in an environment that is too dark, too cold, too small, or else improperly maintained will most probably have a decrease in appetite and may eventually refuse food completely. Be sure to set up and stabilize their habitat before bringing your Kingsnake home, and also monitor it with thermometers, timers, hygrometers, and other helpful equipment.

Using a Separate Feeding Enclosure

In feeding your Kingsnakes, a separate feeding enclosure may not be a requirement in some cases, but it can definitely be helpful. Using a different environment for feeding times can maintain the main enclosure cleaner and more sanitary. A separate feeding enclosure is recommended if you are housing more than one Kingsnake in a habitat, to prevent them from viewing other snakes as prey, and if you utilize a substrate that can be ingested.

When and How Often to Feed California Kingsnake

The time of day when feeding your Kingsnake depends on what time he is most active. Most species of Kingsnakes are nocturnal, therefore should be fed at night.

How often you feed your Kingsnake depends on what species he is as well as how old he is. Baby Kingsnakes won't actually start looking for prey until they are two to four weeks old. Generally, your young snakes need to eat about once every week or so, or depending on how quickly you want them to grow. As your Kingsnake gets older, it will not need to be fed as much. Adult king snakes should be fed once or twice a week.

Pre-Killed vs. Live

Many people who own snakes insist that their pets need the thrill of hunting and catching live prey, such as mice and rats. This is definitely not true. Physical and mental stimulation comes from the overall environment that you create for your Kingsnake, and not from attempting to catch a live prey in a small space.

It is recommended to feed your Kingsnakes pre-killed prey for a number of reasons. They include:

- Live preys can be too active for your baby Kingsnakes

- Attacks that come from live prey can permanently scar and disfigure your Kingsnake.

- There is a large possibility that live prey can attack your Kingsnake, which results to become frightened of it, and it can be very difficult to get that snake to feed him from them on.

- Live prey can fight back during feeding your Kingsnake, causing injuries such as biting through your snake's mouth area, cutting through its tongue's health, and puncturing his eyes.

Therefore, feeding your snake a pre-killed prey is safer, and it will set aside the possibility that the prey may bite and gnaw your snake. What kind of prey you're feeding your Kingsnake will determine how serious an attack can it potentially cause. Generally, mice are harmless for your Kingsnake but rats can actually kill your snake.

If you like to feed your Kingsnakes a live prey, it is recommended that you provide a food source for the prey so it will not try to eat your snake. You have to watch it closely for any signs that it may be gnawing or biting your snake. If ever this will happen, remove the prey immediately and take your Kingsnake to the veterinarian. Remember, the threats that a live prey animal present can be completely eliminated by just feeding pre-killed prey instead!

Pre-killed prey can be bought live and then you can just kill it, or you can buy it already killed. You can freeze pre-killed prey for up to six months. Just be sure to thaw it thoroughly and warm it to slightly above room temperature before feeding it to your Kingsnake.

Tips for Feeding Pre-Killed Prey to your Kingsnake

Your Kingsnake might take immediately to pre-killed prey but if your snake is a little bit picky, the following tips might be helpful:

- Rub the live prey that your Kingsnake prefers against the pre-killed prey before putting in in the terrarium

- Prepare a dish of warm chicken broth and dip the pre-killed prey there.

- Use hemostats or tongs to dangle the prey and "walk" it around the enclosure to make it appear as if the prey is alive and attract the snake to strike at it.

- Make sure that the prey is warmer compared to the room temperature because in that way, it will smell more appetizing to your snake.

- Pierce the braincase of the prey with a nail or a pin to release more appetizing odors.

- Feed your Kingsnake a different colored prey. For example, if you've already tried a white mouse, try switching to a brown mouse instead.

Feeding a California Kingsnake is not easy, but with little effort, time, and the right methods at your fingertips, you can keep you snake happy, healthy, and well-nourished.

California Kingsnake's Diet

- Avoid feeding your Kingsnake wild-caught prey because this can transmit parasites to the snake. The best option is to offer thawed/ frozen rodents, since the freezing process kills any potential parasites the rodents may have.

- You do not need to supplement your Kingsnake's meals with vitamin powders or similar products. Kingsnakes can get all the vitamins and minerals that they need from the food that you feed them, without the need to add anything

- As mentioned above, supplements are not necessary for your Kingsnakes unless your snake has certain medical needs.

- You should always take note that fresh water in a shallow dish must always be available.

- California Kingsnakes aren't picky eaters, so many of them will live their whole lives eating nothing but mice.

- Take into account of using tongs when feeding your California Kingsnake to avoid accidental bites.

- When preparing a pre-killed prey for your pet, thaw it by running it under warm water or setting it in the sun so be sure not to sit it for too long as harmful bacteria can start to form on it.

- Baby Kingsnakes do well eating only one pinky mouse once every week or so.

- Increase the size of the rodent appropriately as your snake grows. A recommended sized meal is one that is no bigger than 1.5 times the width of the snake's body, or leaves only a small lump in the snake's body after being consumed; anything that is too large will result in regurgitation, injuries, seizures, partial paralysis, gut impactions, and death.

- As soon as your California Kingsnake has reached its adult length, you can feed it 1-2 large adult mice every one to two weeks.

- Always remember to feed your snake its prey animals one at a time only and never leave them with live prey unattended for so long especially when your Kingsnake is not hungry as mouse has the tendency to claw, scratch, and bite your snake.

- Be aware that your Kingsnakes can get injured or can sometimes die from prey injuries and bites.

Possible Feeding Problems

A healthy snake should have a healthy appetite, and will eat regularly. But what if they refuse to eat? As long as they are eating, you can be reasonably certain that they are getting sufficient nutrients from their food. A few other possible feeding problems include:

- Refusal of a meal several times in a row
- If your snake regurgitates its meal
- Obvious weight loss
- Signs of disease such as fluid or bubbles in the nostrils, sneezing, or open-mouthed breathing.

If you aren't sure about what you're doing, you can really injure the snake – whether in your handling of them or in how you feed them. Do not force-feed your California Kingsnake just to get him to eat – especially if you do not have experience. Force feeding requires handling the snake while you force food down its throat using tongs or tweezers. It is best to take them to a veterinarian first so that you can identify the cause of your pet's feeding problems.

Chapter Six: California Kingsnake Husbandry

Snake keepers use the term "husbandry" to refer to the regular and daily care of a pet snake. Two of the most important facets of snake husbandry have already been discussed in the previous chapters: housing and feeding. In this chapter, we take a look at some of the other aspects types of husbandry care and maintenance that you will need to do to make sure that your California Kingsnake is kept clean, safe, and in good health.

Cleaning and Disinfecting the Snake Cage and Habitat

Aside from providing appropriate heating, lighting, humidity, and cage structures and décor, you will also want to clean your California Kingsnake's habitat enclosure regularly. This is particularly important as the prevailing humidity within the enclosure can be a perfect ground for the growth of bacteria. Most reptiles can be prone to skin and bacterial infection if left alone in unclean surroundings for long.

Regular cage maintenance and cleaning should be part of your routine. Not only will this keep the interior of the enclosure clean, odor-free, and healthy, but it will also keep you and your family safe and healthy. Regular cleaning prevents the possible transmission of diseases like Salmonella, which can be found in the fecal matter of reptiles, and which may be transmissible to humans.

Spot cleaning the interior of the cage should be done as often as possible – at least once a day, or once every other day. Spot cleaning your reptile's cage can include:

- The removal of fecal matter as soon as you notice them
- The removal of shed skin
- The removal of uneaten food

- Cleaning and refilling the water bowls at least twice a week

A more thorough cage cleaning should be done at least once a month, ideally more. During this process, you will need to relocate the snake so that you can clean and sterilize the entire cage components, including perches, decorations, substrate, etc. To be able to do this thoroughly, you will need to temporarily relocate your Kingsnake to a different holding cage or cell. As usual, make sure that this cage is secure and clean, and is sufficiently ventilated.

- **Remove all of the cage items, disposing directly of the substrate which you will be replacing completely.**

Set aside these cage items in a bowl or container. You will now proceed to clean the inside of the terrarium or cage, and then later on to disinfect and sterilize the cage items. Gather the following materials to help you in your cleaning tasks:

- A spray bottle
- Brushes, Q-tips, putty knives, or razor blades
- Buckets
- Terrarium cleaner that is safe for reptiles
- Paper towels
- Robber gloves
- Sponges

- **Learn to unplug everything!**

Make sure that all the electrical components of the cage – such as heating and lighting, are turned off or unplugged. Then armed with a spray bottle, a sponge, gloves, and just regular soap and water, begin to clean the interior of the snake cage as thoroughly as possible. Make use of instruments such as brushes, Q-tips, putty knives, or razor blades to really get at the hardened feces or waste that a regular paper towel won't be able to dislodge. Really get into it, using herp-safe terrarium cleaners for the really troublesome spots and corners. Rinse the inside of the cage thoroughly.

- **Clean and disinfect the cage items by boiling them in water for some 30 minutes.**

The only way to be sure is to kill any thriving bacteria through high heat and boiling temperatures as you thoroughly sterilize each cage item. Try to avoid using regular household chemical cleaners which may prove toxic or harmful to your pet. Besides, even using these types of cleansers cannot really guarantee the thorough elimination of bacteria.

Use a disinfectant to give another through cleaning to all the cage items, including the interior of the snake cage. Then use hot water to rinse of all chemical residues. Allow it all to air-dry, making sure that the cage interior and all the various cage items and implements are thoroughly dried.

- **Reinstall cage items inside**

After doing the steps above, reinstall all the cage items and decorations, this time putting on a new layer of fresh substrate. You might also want to give your California Kingsnake a bath before allowing it to return to its newly cleaned and dry terrarium.

Wash and disinfect all your cleaning tools and equipment with the same thoroughness that you practiced when you were cleaning the cage interior and the cage items. And finally, wash your hands thoroughly – using hot, soapy water. Don't forget to finish off with a disinfectant, too.

Tips for Bathing a California Kingsnake

Bathing a pet snake is a simple and straightforward process – but with loads of benefits for your pet. An occasional bath for your California Kingsnake can therefore go a long way to having a happy and healthy snake. Bathing can help relieve constipation in your snake, and it can also kill mites and promotes shedding.

Use warm spring or filtered water. Don't use tap or chlorinated water as the chemicals in the water can actually irritate their skin. A good range between 100 and 105 degrees Fahrenheit is a good level for a snake bath. And because they are sensitive to temperature changes, you'll want to provide them with a reasonably warm bath.

You can help your snake get into the bath, but more often than not, they will quickly bathe themselves. You don't want your California Kingsnake getting away from you during bathing time; you might want to place a sufficiently roomy bowl of the warm bath water in an enclosure.

Just let your California Kingsnake swim freely around in the water. If it shows signs of agitation, take it out immediately. Otherwise, let it soak around for 10 to 15 minutes. When it is done, pick it up, gently use a towel to dry it off, and then return it to his now clean, sterilized, disinfected, and thoroughly dried habitat.

Some recommend placing your snake in a holding cage immediately after a bath as some snakes can defecate immediately after a bath, and you don't want him doing this too soon within the newly cleaned cage. Give your California Kingsnake sufficient time in the holding cage to do his business before moving him back to his home.

Chapter Seven: Caring Guidelines for California Kingsnake

California Kingsnake can be great pets for those who take time to learn on how to properly take care of them.

This chapter will give you a whole lot of tips on to be a great owner of a California Kingsnake including points on how to properly tame them, handle them, and introduce them to people or other house pets as well. These things are essential in making your pet's lifestyle as fun and wonderful as it can be. It'll make you a better owner if you know your snake's strength and weaknesses.

Tips on How to Tame your California Kingsnake

- When you get your new Kingsnake, just leave it for about five days or weeks or so that it can get used to its surroundings because when you get a new snake, it's going to be a little bit feisty. They won't feel like it's a high more secure surrounding.

- Make sure that you give your Kingsnake a plenty of hides because if it's out and if you'll give them a lot of space, it's not going to feel safe for them because in the wild, they will go hide under the rocks, bushes, or wherever.

- If you feed your Kingsnake, don't handle it for at least 24 hours after feeding the snake. Give them time to digest their food because it is not a good idea if you handle it straight after you feed it.

- When you feed your Kingsnake, feed it out of its enclosure so that when the owner put his hand on the snake's cage, it won't think that the hand is a food; thus, preventing to be bitten by your snake.

- Another top tip when you want to handle and tame your California Kingsnake is to just put and leave your hand on its cage so it gets used to your hand. In that way, your Kingsnake will know that your hand is not food and won't try to hurt you.

Introducing Yourself to your Kingsnake

Give your Kingsnake time to adjust to you

Whether it's a hatchling or captive-bred Kingsnake that shows little aggression, or with a great deal of aggressive behavior, the first thing you should consider is to allow your Kingsnake to adjust to you. Let's say, for the first week or so, just sit outside its terrarium for about an hour each day and allow it to get used to your smell. Never attempt to touch your Kingsnake during these first few weeks.

Move items around in its terrarium without touching it

At the end of this initial week, you can now begin to move things around inside your Kingsnake's terrarium. However, it is still not allowed to attempt to touch your Kingsnake at this point. Continuously do this for another week so that your Kingsnake can get used to the idea that you have no intention to harm him. Being around it without attempting to touch it will let your Kingsnake know that you are not a danger or threat.

Touch your snake inside its cage

Once you think that your snake know that you are not a threat, you can start to touch it while inside its cage by placing your hand in its cage and gently start touching it, moving it around inside the cage, and lifting your snake's tail. Continue doing this manner to your snake for three to four days.

Dealing with your Kingsnake's Aggressive Behavior

Determine why it is aggressive

Unless you're taming a Kingsnake hatchling or captive-bred Kingsnake, you'll likely have to deprogram your snake's aggressive behavior. The first thing to do is to know what type of aggression your Kingsnake is showing. There are two types of aggressive responses you can deprogram your Kingsnake – territorial, or defensive responses, and feeding responses.

- Territorial responses are instinctive and not an expression of aggressions. Snakes live most of their lives in fear of being eaten by bigger predators, including humans, so this kind of response is more of a defense mechanism which can be tamed with gentle and consistent care.

- Feeding responses, on the other hand, are also natural, instinctive response. Generally, snakes are taught to bite whatever comes into their terrarium. Since they assume that anything that comes to their cage is food, you might get bitten if you put your hand inside without first deprogramming this aggressive response.

"Hook train" especially aggressive Kingsnakes

Some species of Kingsnakes are more aggressive than others and might be requiring more training. If you're dealing with a particularly aggressive type of Kingsnake, you might consider to "hook train" it. You can do this by gently rubbing its body or pushing down on its head with a hook, or a similar inanimate object, evey time you go to get it out of its cage. By doing this, your Kingsnake will be able to know it is not yet feeding time so there is no need to bite whatever enters its terrarium.

- If your Kingsnake appears to be scared whenever you open its terrarium, spend a little more time rubbing its body with the hook until it will calm down. For example, if your snake coils into a ball, flattens out its body, or pose a striking position, spend some time rubbing its body until it will come to a point that it will relax a bit.

- Start rubbing your Kingsnake's body down from its tail end and up to its head. It could seem threatening if you start it with its head especially if your snake is already scared.

Hold your snake more often than you feed it

The very most common reason why people get bitten by their pet snake is because their snake is reacting to its feeding response every time something enters its terrarium. To handle this kind of response, stop feeding your Kingsnake every week. Instead, feed it only once every three weeks, but be sure to handle your snake every day. This will deprogram your Kingsnake from thinking that everything that enters its terrarium is food.

- It can also be useful to feed your snake in a separate tub. This will also help it from thinking that everything that comes to its terrarium is food. But don't feed it only in the tub because this will just transfer its response from the terrarium to the tub.

- It is safe to only feed your Kingsnake once every three weeks since Kingsnakes can go weeks without eating, with any harm done.

Handling your Kingsnake Properly

- **Be confident**

After introducing yourself to your snake, and have worked on handling it of any aggressive behavior, you can now begin to handle your snake outside its cage. It is very vital that you handle your snake with confidence. If you are still fearful or hesitant, your snake will be able to sens it and act the same way.

It is a nice idea to handle your Kingsnake under the supervision of a professional or long-time owner before actually getting one for yourself. This will guarantee that you are comfortable with your Kingsnake when you get it.

- **Wash your hands**

You should always wash your hands thoroughly before handling your Kingsnake. Snakes have an excellent sensory organ so if they smell a scent of prey on your hand, your Kingsnake might mistake your hand for something it should eat.

Also, washing your hands before handling your Kingsnake helps prevent any foreign bacteria, germs, or parasites in your pet's environment.

- **Provide support for its body**

It is very vital to support your Kingsnake's body when you are picking or handling it up so that it is comfortable with you and there is no strain put on its body. This is true whether you are picking your Kingsnake up with your hands or with a hook. Keep the first third of your snake's body supported with either the hook or one of your hands, while supporting the back two thirds of your Kingsnake's body with your other arm.

Keep in mind your "hook training" before putting your hands in your Kingsnake's terrarium. Lightly pressing down on your Kingsnake's head with a hook will give the snake an idea that it is not feeding time so there is no need to strike. Never grab your Kingsnake by the end of its tail to pick it up or move it. This can cause serious strain and fear to your Kingsnake.

- **Never restrain its head**

Restraining your Kingsnake's head can make it believe that you are a predator that's trying to hurt the snake. Whenever you handle your Kingsnake, stick to holding it by its body, and avoid holding or restraining its head.

- **Point its head away from you**

Until you know within yourself that you can properly handle your snake, it is a good idea to hold it with its head facing away from you. This will give your Kingsnake a chance to become familiarized to you and the motion of your hands or body without the danger that the experience may turn negative.

Creating the Right Environment for your California Kingsnake

- **Get the right cage size**

If your Kingsnake is still showing aggressive behavior after you have introduced yourself and deprogrammed it, there could be something on its environment that makes it upset or sick. If your Kingsnake feels upset because it is too cold or hot, or feels threatened or vulnerable in its environment, it is more likely to lash out. Thus, creating and maintaining a right environment for your pet is imperative to taming it. Getting it a proper cage is the first step in creating the environment of your Kingsnake. California Kingsnakes need a 30 to 55 gallon tank.

- **Provide proper lighting**

California Kingsnakes are diurnal snakes, thus, they need a bright white light during the day and very dim lighting during the night. You have to place an incandescent white light above your Kingsnake's terrarium if the room you are keeping your snake in has only dim lighting. In this way, you can give them enough light. On the other hand, they need very little light during the night. Decorative incandescent lights that come in dark colors such as red, blue, and green will give the right amount of light during the night.

Heating and lighting your Kingsnake's cage go hand in hand so you may want to pay attention to how one affects the other

- **Provide a primary heat source**

Kingsnakes require the right temperature to live comfortably. This means they require both a primary and secondary heat source. Primary heat source is needed to keep the temperature of the entire terrarium in the correct range. You can do this by adding a series of incandescent lights along the top of the terrarium.

Generally, Kinsnakes prefer a temperature that ranges from 80 to 88 degrees Fahrenheit (26 to 31 degrees Cecius)

However, at night, it is most recommended that the temperature will be held at 5 to 20 degrees cooler than their daytime temperature.

There are a lot of varieties to create the right night time temperature on your Kingsnake's terrarium. You can use different options such as a heating pad placed under the snake's terrarium, ceramic infrared heat emitters, or nocturnal reptile incandescent light bulbs. All of these things that were mention provide heat without much light

Use several thermometers and place it in your Kingsnake's terrarium to ensure that you are keeping it at optimal temperatures.

- **Provide a secondary heat source**

Snakes need a temperature gradient in their terrariums so that they can go to whichever temperature is most comfortable for them. You can do this by installing a secondary heat source in your Kingsnake's terrarium. The secondary heat source must only cover 25 to 30 percent, approximately, of the terrarium of your snake.

In order to create this secondary heat source, you can either place an under-the tank-heater underneath only one-quarter of the tank or you can mount a 50 to 75 watt incandescent light bulb located on the outside of one wall of the snake's terrarium.

"Basking lights" are a very great choice to create a heat gradient as well. Basking lights are placed outside the terrarium wherein it creates heat in one specific area of the tank.

- **Create various hiding places for your Kingsnake**

Snakes are hiders by nature, especially when they are in the wild. They often hide if they feel threatened so if you do not have places for them to hide, it will likely feel threatened and vulnerable, thus, resulting to an aggressive behavior.

Great hiding places may be a cave made of rock or a clean piece of cardboard. You can also be creative and use plastic or clay flowerpots as their hiding places.

- **Provide water**

Just like any other animals, Kingsnakes need water in order to survive. Be sure that your pet snake has clean and fresh water all the time. You can use a water bowl in its terrarium, but make sure it is not easily tipped over.

Important Reminder

- Do not handle a Kingsnake if it's shedding because they might be more aggressive during these times.

- You can still expect your Kingsnake to exhibit some defensive behavior even though they are tamed. These behaviors include emitting a foul-smelling odor, musking, thrashing, or biting. However, these actions are not dangerous since Kingsnakes are non-venomous snakes and don't normally cause any serious injury.

Chapter Eight: Breeding Your California Kingsnake

At this point, you might be excited in breeding your California Kingsnake. But take in consideration that before attempting to breed your snake, it is important to ensure that they are in good health, with good body weight and no ailments. Breeding Kingsnakes may sound fun but it should be taken seriously.

This chapter is enticed with lots of information about breeding your California Kingsnake. It will give you fully loaded information about the processes that takes place in breeding snakes as well as tips on how to breed them. Some people are born to be breeders so this chapter is definitely for you, so continue reading on!

Sexing

A successful breeding program begins with a healthy breeding pair. Females usually reach sexual maturity after 31 months, while the sexual maturity of males occurs after 18 years. The process by which you can identify whether a snake is a male or a female is called sexing.

Sexing can be done in either one of two ways: by cloacal popping or cloacal probing. Please take note that you should never sex hatchlings. They are very sensitive and delicate at this stage, and attempting to sex them can injure them severely.

Cloacal popping is done by applying pressure with the thumb just below the vent. This will cause the hemipenes of a male to avert, one on each side of the cloacal opening. Females, on the other hand, may avert her cloaca and erect her scent gland papillae.

Cloacal probing is the more commonly employed means of sexing. It is done by gently inserting a lubricated probe – a slender stainless steel – into the side of the vent, and then sliding them into the pockets that are found on either side of the tail. For males, the probe will slide to a depth of approximately 10 scales, while for a female; it will go for only 3 or 4 scales. Sometimes the probe will only go somewhere between these two ranges, and these are often classified as unsexed snakes. Probing isn't always definitive or certain, and other factors may influence the result such as the pressure you exert on the probe, or something blocking the pockets so you could not insert the probe deep enough. It is essential that you don't try to attempt to probe your snake if you do not have sufficient experience with sexing. A mistake here can injure and damage your snake, and there is always the chance that the results of your probe can be wrong.

More often than not, a determination of a snake's sex can be established from their behavior. Males are generally more active than females. They also tend to refuse food during breeding time. But perhaps the best sign that your snake is a male is when he averts his hemipenes when he is defecating. When he sheds his skin, the hemipenes can be identified as two dried bits of skin at the vent – but which should not be confused with a small bump that can also show in the shed skin of females. Their tail shape can also differ, with the male's being more parallel and bulbous, as opposed to the female's tail which is more tapered in shape.

For a breeding pair, females should ideally be bigger and weightier than males. This is to allow them to have sufficient body weight that can undergo the stress of egg production. Females are usually paired only after they have reached 1,200 to 1,500 grams, which they can reach around the age of 3 or 4 years. Males, on the other hand, can be a lot younger and lighter; some use males that have reached 50 to

700 grams. The selected breeding pair must both be in good health, with good body weight and muscle tone.

Brumation

Brumation is the term called for the cooling period that takes place in order to successfully breed Kingsnakes. The first thing to do to breed Kingsnakes is to start increasing their feeding pattern in late April in order to give your snake an extra fat reserves that they will be needing during brumation. Keep your heaters on in the month of May but cease feeding the snakes for at least 2-3 weeks before you cool them down so that the Kingsnakes can empty their digestive tracks. During brumation, any food leftover will rot in your Kingsnake's stomach which then leads to a deadly infection.

In the month of June, you have to drop your Kingsnake's cage temperatures from 10-15 degrees Celsius in a span of 2-3 months. The brumation temperatures can be slightly higher or lower than this. In early September, you can now begin to slowly return back your Kingsnake's summer temperature. Never heat your Kingsnakes up to quickly because this can affect your male snake's fertility.

Mating

Shedding of female Kingsnakes will take place two weeks after they come out of brumation. This is called the post-brumation shed which shows that your female Kingsnake is ready to mate. Introduce your male Kingsnake into the female Kingsnake's terrarium. If the female is receptive, mating behavior will start immediately and the male Kingsnake will mate with the female one very soon. Mating can last for a few minutes to a few hours.

Be sure to separate the two Kingsnakes after they finished mating because they can be cannibalistic. To increase the chance of fertile eggs, allow your Kingsnakes to mate more than once.

Egg Laying

Female Kingsnakes will undergo a pre-laying shed for four to six weeks after successful mating. Ten to fourteen days after the pre-laying shed, the female Kingsnake will lay her eggs. You have to provide a laying box filled with moist sphagnum moss for your Kingsnake to lay its eggs in. Expect that your female Kingsnake will spend a lot of time in the egg laying box prior to laying eggs. You have to take note also to check the egg laying box as often as possible for eggs. Kingsnakes can lay approximately 6-20 eggs but clutches are usually smaller than 20. The size of the female egg is dependent on the number of eggs a Kingsnake will lay, meaning the larger the Female Kingsnake, the more the number of eggs it will lay. You have to move the eggs into an incubator once your Kingsnake has finished laying all its eggs.

Egg Incubation

You need to incubate your Kingsnake's eggs on a moist incubation container because snake eggs have a leathery shell which absorbs moisture throughout the incubation period. You can place your Kingsnake's eggs in a plastic container filled with a layer of perlite a few centimeters deep. Mix the perlite with water at a ratio of 1 part perlite to 1 part water by weight. You may need to add more water to the incubation container if the Kingsnake's eggs start to dent during incubation. You can also use vermiculite to incubate your Kingsnake's eggs.

Do not put air holes in the incubation container. Just open the lid for a few minutes a few times every week to allow air to enter. It is very vital not to turn the Kingsnake's eggs and keep them in the position that they were laid in or else the embryo will detach from the shell and die. Incubation of Kingsnake's eggs ranges from 27-28 degrees Celsius. They will hatch in approximately 60 days with this kind of temperature.

Hatchling

Baby Kingsnake have an egg tooth that they use to slit open the egg shell. When you already see some slits appearing on your eggs, it means that the eggs are hatching. Eventually, you will see the baby Kingsnakes poking their heads out of the eggs. You have to wait for several days for the entire clutch to hatch. Never attempt to remove the baby Kingsnakes from the eggs. Just allow them to hatch on their own. As soon as the baby Kingsnakes have hatched, remove them from the incubation container and place them separately in individual plastic tubs.

Breeding Groups

For a basic breeding group, it is recommended to purchase two male Kingsnakes and four female Kingsnakes, as unrelated as possible, unless there is a certain genetic trait that you want to isolate and work with. If they all grow to maturity, you will be having two trios. When the time comes that you need to sell or pick for future generations of breeders, you can mix from the two unrelated trios. If ever something happened to your first male, your second male can breed to all four females. On the other hand, if one female "goes down" you still are in production.

Make sure that the Kingsnakes are sexed correctly. You can check it by yourself, or you can have the breeder confirm the sex and show you how. There is a usual mistake that a male is wrongly categorized as female because the hemipenes do not "pop" when checked. You can always double check with a probe. I guess you do not want to raise your snakes in a long period of time only to find out some females are males.

Checking for Sperm and Follicles

You can use a microscope to check for sperm. Take the seminal plug on a mount, add some saline solution if needed (solution used for contact lens also works), and put it under a microscope on shaded screen a 200 power. By then, you have to see a lot of sperm swimming. If not, you may want to use your second male.

Sometimes, it is preferred to use a Calci-Sand because you can see the seminal plug on the sand if your miss the actual mating. In that case, you can gently squeeze a little fluid from the mated female Kingsnake and have a sperm check. You can find a few live sperm up to a week after confirmed mating, but the sooner you test, the better.

Usually, when a female Kingsnake is ready to breed, you can touch and feel her follicles. You can gently indent your thumb up into their rib cage about mid-body, and just let the snake crawl over your thumb. In this way, you can feel bumps like soft marbles. These are the ones that are developed into eggs when fertilized. You should always have the male be with the female at this to,e/

Taking Care of a Pregnant Snake

Number one thing we need to do if we have a pregnant snake is that we should observe privacy. Snakes are very, very shy and in times like that, it's a great idea to observe them from afar. Our pet Kingsnakes will lay eggs so it's very important that there will be an incubation area and a laying area which is very easy to do. You can use sphagnum moss, peat moss, vermiculite, and what they will just do is they will burrow down in the vermiculite. You have to take note that the substrate should stay moist but not wet. You'll get hatchlings quicker at higher temperatures but you will also get more congenital defects.

Those defects normally show up not only in immune problems, but in different patterns of color.

Raising Young California Kingsnakes

It is preferred to raise baby Kingsnakes to a clear, plastic shoebox rack system. Baby Kingsnakes are usually kept in the standard shoebox during the first year. The floor of the cage should have a heat that may be provided by heat tape toward the rear, with the thermostat set at 84 degrees Farenheit and a background temperature that ranges in the mid-70s, so the snake can thermo-regulate.

Each shoebox should have a snake record card taped on the lid. You can use fine, kiln-fried pine shavings as substrate and you have to provide a lightweight water bowl for each baby. If ever you think of using a heavy water bowl, you have to assure it's resting on the cage floor. If there is a substrate underneath, it may attempt to burrow and crush itself. If you keep baby Kingsnakes together, one may kill and swallow its cage mate, which result to death in the process.

You can offer two, three, or even four meals every week to your baby Kingsnakes because there is no possibility that they may be overfed. You have to make sure to use size-appropriate prey. Each meal has to leave a small but noticeable lump in the Kingsnake's body. If your baby Kingsnakes keep and accept their meals down, they will definitely grow rapidly. Size is the important thing when it comes to sexual maturity and not age. Not all Kingsnakes accept food and grow fast, but as long as they are getting long, not fat, it will be fine. Once they are nearing their adult size, and starting to get fat, you have to slow down on the food, unless you want overweight breeder snakes, which is not appropriate.

If your Kingsnakes always accept food all year, feed them through the first winter. If they refuse food during the winter but might seem healthy, you need to brumate them.

The terrarium must be dry, but should have drinking water available. It at some point gets too humid, consider a covered water bowl, or remove the bowl for a few days. If the ventilation holes in the box can't keep up with the humidity caused by feces, or if ever you have to clean the box at all times, it is recommended to move the Kingsnake up to a sweater box, and for smaller species, a breeder cage.

Chapter Nine: Keeping Your California Snake Healthy

You as the owner should be aware of the potential threats and diseases that could harm the wellness of your California Kingsnake. Just like human beings, you need to have knowledge on these diseases so that you can prevent it from happening in the first place. You will find tons of information on the most common problems that may affect your California Kingsnake including its causes, signs and symptoms, remedies and prevention. While you may not be able to prevent your rabbit from getting sick in certain situations, you can be responsible in educating yourself about the diseases that could affect your California Kingsnake.

The more you know about these potential health problems, the better you will be able to identify them and to seek immediate veterinary care when needed.

Common Health Problems Affecting California Kingsnake

Snakes can be affected by a number of different health problems and they are generally not specific to any particular breed. Feeding your California Kingsnake a nutritious diet will go a long way in securing his total health and wellbeing, but sometimes snakes get ill anyway. If you want to make sure that your snake gets the treatment he needs as quickly as possible you need to learn how to identify the symptoms of disease. These symptoms are not always obvious either; your California Kingsnake may not show any outward signs of illness except for a subtle change in behavior.

The more time you spend with your pet snake, the more you will come to understand his behavior – this is the key to catching health problems early. At the first sign that something is wrong with your snake you should take inventory of his symptoms – both physical and behavioral – so you can relay them to your veterinarian who will then make a diagnosis and prescribe a course of treatment. The sooner you identify these symptoms, the sooner your vet can take action and the more likely your California Kingsnake will be able to make a full recovery.

California Kingsnake can be prone to a wide variety of different diseases or infections, though some are more common than others. For the benefit your California Kingsnake's long-term health, take the time to learn the causes, symptoms, and treatment options for some of the most common health problems.

Below are some of the most common health problems that can occur to California Kingsnake. You will learn some guidelines on how these diseases can be prevented and treated as well as its signs and symptoms.

Constipation

Constipation is a common problem among captive snakes such as the Kingsnake. Its causes include suboptimal environmental temperature, illness, injuries, dehydration, parasitism, and cloacoliths. Constipated snakes must be allowed to soak in very warm water for 20-30 minutes daily for 1-2 days. By doing this, your snake can defecate or urinate. You should see a vet if this conservative measure is not successful.

Cloacoliths

Dehydration of captive Kingsnakes may result in drying out their urinary excretions. If this occurs, uric acid "stones" tend to form within cloaca ('cloacoloths'). This prevents them from expulsion of urinary waste and feces, which creates serious illness. Dehydration is not a disease itself but a sign of disease, so it becomes the vet's task to determine the underlying problem that caused the dehydration. Cloacoliths can often be manually expelled with patience and the help of mineral oil enemas. Only an experienced vet must attempt this procedure.

Prolapses

A prolapsed happens when an organ inverts itself inside out and protrudes through the usual external opening of that organelle. Prolapses of the cloaca and reproductive organs are common among captive snakes like the Kingsnakes. The cause can still not be determined.

Abnormal shedding

This occurs when the normal sequence of events of the shedding process is somehow interrupted. It usually results in a piece-meal shed or retained eye caps. The causes of this include inadequate relative humidity, serious internal disease, previous injury to the scales and skin, external parasitism, lack of adequate objects against which to rub at the beginning of the shed and thyroid gland problems.

Retaine Eye Caps

Retained eye caps are often a manifestation of an abnormal shed. The eye caps serve as the outermost cellular layers of the corneas, which are supposed to be shed each time the outermost layers of the skin are shed. Take note that only experienced vet must attempt to carefully remove the corneal remnants.

Respiratory Infections

California Kingsnakes are often infected by respiratory tract, like colds and pneumonia. The cause of these colds is a suboptimal temperature in the snake's enclosure. If you observe that your snake emits a wheezing sound when breathing, or holds its head up and mouth open, you should immediately seek veterinarian assistance.

Stress in Snakes

The most common causes of stress in snakes come from having no place to hide, feeling threatened, being handled too often or improperly, and living in substandard conditions. The good thing about this is that most of these factors can be greatly reduced simply by providing the proper care for your snake. You cannot easily observe stress in snakes the way you can see other health problems, like external parasites or a retained shred. Stress can build up in snakes to result to other symptoms such as the refusal to eat, weight loss, lethargy, and in extreme cases, even death. So you have to find ways to reduce stress and understand what causes it, if you want to lengthen your snake's life.

Failure to Voluntarily Feed (Anorexia)

Failure to voluntarily feed and lack of appetite are common problems among captive snakes. The owner must make every attempt to discover the reasons for the snake's failure to feed despite the fact that snakes are uniquely suited to survive prolonged periods without feeding.

Regurgitation

This may outcome from handling a snake too soon after it is fed. Regurgitated food is generally odorless and undigested. Another cause of this is inadequate and incomplete digestion caused that is caused by cool environmental temperatures. In these cases, the food appears digested and is malodorous. If it is not possible to raise the temperature of the terrarium, a focal source of heat where the snake can rest is needed to ensure adequate and complete digestion. Other causes of this are stress, parasitism, serious internal disease, and intestinal obstruction. It is recommended that an experienced vet must be consulted if the cause is not determined.

Burns

Snakes can get their burns from unprotected or malfunctioning heat lamps or other heat sources. The fact is, snakes do not tend to move away from the heat source that causes the injury, thus, making the wounds considerably more serious. Medical treatments for this are injectable antibiotics and periodic wound dressing. Surgery may also be needed to minimize the disfiguring effects of such injuries. These injuries can be avoided by periodically checking all heating appliances to make certain that they are functioning well and they are "snake proof."

Rat/Mouse Attack

A live mouse or rat may sometimes injure your Kingsnake while fighting for its life. Veterinary action should be sought for serious bite wounds.

Rostral Abrasions

Due to captivity, captive animals tend to injure themselves from repeated attempts to escape. Snakes tend to rub and push their noses against the walls of their terrarium as they search of a means to escape. This can cause damages to their scales and skin of the nose. If the trauma continues, it may result to deep ulceration of the rostrum with subsequent deformity. It can be difficult to prevent this problem, but adequate hiding places and other additions to the terrarium such as artificial plants, branches, etc, can help minimize it.

Abscesses

This is a common form of bacterial infection among snakes. They can be external, in which results from bite wounds and other injuries to the skin or it can also be internal, which may be located within one or more organs and within the body cavity. A vet can be helpful to surgically open and flush external abscesses. The abscess cavity can be treated with topical antibiotics but abscesses within the body are not accessible for treatment.

Parasitic diseases

Parasites that are eaten by snakes can cause many problems. For example, protozoa can cause serious diseases in the respiratory, digestive, reproductive and vascular blood and bloodstream in snakes. Large numbers of ticks and mites parasitize the skin and scales of a snake, and can create disease by feeding on the host's blood.

Blister Disease

Blister disease is common in many captive snakes. It is often associated with the maintenance of these animals in damp, filthy environments. The first sign of this disease is usually a red or pink appearance of the bottom-most scales. Soon, these scales become infected and swollen by bacteria and fungi. At the first suspicion of this disease, you have to ask for veterinary help. Treatment involves use of topical and injectable antibiotics. Furthermore, the underlying hygiene and sanitation problems must be corrected. This disease can be prevented if you are aware of it and if the enclosure in which captive snakes are housed is kept dry and scrupulously clean.

Septicemia

A wide variety of bacteria can cause septicemia, or generalized internal infections. These bacteria may invade they body of the snake by way of wounds and abscesses or as a consequence of serious illness originally localized in the respiratory, gastrointestinal and reproductive tracts. Signs include anorexia, lethargy, dehydration and regurgitation of incompletely digested food, redness to the skin and scales, or bleeding from the skin. The assistance of an experienced veterinarian is essential in these cases. The outlook for the snakes with this kind of disease is always guarded to poor.

The attending vet may collect a specimen for bacterial culture and antibiotic sensitivity testing, as well as one or more blood sample so that it can be accurately determined the extent of the disease, whether or not various internal organs are involved. Treatment for this disease includes injectable antibiotics and appropriate supportive care. Treatment is usually long-term and periodic monitoring for the snake's status is very important for a favorable outcome.

Signs of Possible Illnesses

- **Eating Disorders** – does your snake show signs of appetite loss?
- **Skin** - does its skin peeling off abnormally? If your snake is ill or infected, it appears physically on its body and can have a poor skin condition or hair loss.
- **Mobility** – does your snake swiftly move? Or does it have trouble moving from one place to another?
- **Eyes** - are there any discharge in the eyes? Is it swelling? Is it not bright or clear?

California Kingsnake Care Sheet

Congratulate yourself! You are now on your way to becoming a very well-informed and pro-active California Kingsnake owner! Finishing this book is a huge milestone for you and your future or present pet, but before this ultimate guide comes to a conclusion, keep in mind the most important things you have acquired through reading this book.

This chapter will outline the summary of what you have learned, including the checklist you need to keep in mind to ensure that you and your California Kingsnake lived happily ever after!

Basic Information

Scientific Name: *Lampropeltis getula californiae*

Breed Size as they hatch from their eggs: 8 to 12 inches

Average size: 3 to 4 feet

Maximum adult size: more than six feet

Caging: bigger is better

Food: mice, rat, bird, rattlesnake, live chickens etc.

Skin Pattern: banded or striped

Color: Range between black and brown with white or yellow markings

Temperament: docile and calm; can be at times aggressive

Health Conditions: have no special health requirements aside from normal snake diseases and health concerns

Wild Diet: Feeds largely but not exclusively on other snakes. They also eat birds, rodents, lizards and have the ability to consume rattlesnakes with no apparent ill effect

Museum Diet: Mice and small rats.

Life Span in the Wild: 10 to 15 years

Life Span in Captivity: 15 to 20 years

Overall Lifespan: average 20 to 35 years

Habitat Requirements

Recommended Equipment: Terrarium or snake cage/enclosure, water bowl, substrate, plants, driftwood, moss, and rocks, heat and light sources, thermometer, thermostat, light timer

Recommended Day/Light Cycle: 12-12 hours

Recommended Temperature: 80-85 degrees Fahrenheit

Recommended Humidity Levels: 50 percent

Cleaning Frequency: Daily cage cleaning with weekly maintenance, and everything put into the cage should be washed and disinfected weekly as well.

Nutritional Needs

Primary Diet: small rodents, eggs, small birds and fish, snakes and lizards, frogs, small mammals

Feeding Frequency (Hatchlings): once a week

Feeding Frequency (Juvenile): once or twice a week

Feeding Frequency (Adult): once every 1-2 weeks

Water: Fresh water in a bowl should be always available.

Breeding Information

Age of Sexual Maturity (Females): 27 to 31 months

Age of Sexual Maturity (Males): 16 to 18 months

Copulation: 2 to 3 days

Courtship: begins in the spring

Mating Period: few minutes to a few hours

Gestation Period: 60 days

Ovulation: Swelling at the last third of the body that lasts for about 12 to 24 hours. A pre-lay shed will follow approximately 15 days later.

Egg Laying: Approximately 28 days after the pre-lay shed.

Clutch Size: 5-12 eggs with an average of nine

Birth Interval: 15 – 30 minutes

Recommended Incubation Temperatures: 80 to 84 degrees Fahrenheit

Recommended Incubation Humidity Levels: 90 to 100 percent

Length at Birth: 20 to 30 cm

Weight at Birth: 65 to 103 grams

Index

Photo Credits

Page 1 Photo by user Jack Goldfarb via Flickr.com
<https://www.flickr.com/photos/the_horned_jew_lizard/457
3957792/ >

Page 12 Photo by user Ross Padilla via Flickr.com,
<https://www.flickr.com/photos/deserthunterscal_kings/687
8905342/>

Page 20 Photo by user Ross Padilla via Flickr.com,
<https://www.flickr.com/photos/deserthunterscal_kings/689
8154380/>

Page 35 Photo by user Ross Padilla via Flickr.com,
<https://www.flickr.com/photos/deserthunterscal_kings/704
4252339>

Page 48 Photo by user Edward Astudillo via Flickr.com,
<https://www.flickr.com/photos/150678474@N04/3261772173
6>

Page 56 Photo by user Jack Goldfarb via Flickr.com,
<https://www.flickr.com/photos/the_horned_jew_lizard/281
5525637>

Page 69 Photo by user Ross Padilla via Flickr.com,
<https://www.flickr.com/photos/deserthunterscal_kings/6898154722/>

Page 75 Photo by user California Reptile and Amphibian via Flickr.com,
<https://www.flickr.com/photos/64527132@N06/9082675026/>
Page 88 Photo by user Devin Bergquist via Flickr.com
<https://www.flickr.com/photos/123633208@N05/1651599829>

Page 99 Photo by user Calibas via Wikimedia Commons
<https://commons.wikimedia.org/wiki/File:Californiakingsnake.jpg>

Page 109 Photo by user Pierre Fidenci via Wikimedia Commons

<https://commons.wikimedia.org/wiki/File:Lampropeltis_getulus04.jpg>

References

"10 Facts about California King Snakes" SnakesAliveUK
<https://snakesaliveuk.wordpress.com/2013/01/16/10-facts-about-california-king-snakes/>

"All Hail the California Kingsnake"
By Maria Heidkamp Scully, Reptiles Magazine
<http://www.reptilesmagazine.com/Snakes/Snake-Care/All-Hail-The-California-Kingsnake/>

"California Kingsnake - Lampropeltis californiae"
PetMd.com
<http://www.petmd.com/reptile/species/california-kingsnake>

"Choosing a Pet Snake" Lianne McLeod, DVM.
<http://exoticpets.about.com/cs/snakes/a/snakesaspets.htm>

"Controlled Exotic Snake Permit" TPWD Texas
<http://tpwd.texas.gov/faq/business/permits/nonindigenous_snakes/index.phtml>

"How to Tame Snakes" Wikihow.com
<http://www.wikihow.com/Tame-Snakes>

"Kingsnake Facts" LiveScience.com
<http://www.livescience.com/53890-kingsnake.html

"**Snake Feeding Tips**" DrsFosterSmith.com
<http://www.drsfostersmith.com/pic/article.cfm?c=6016&arti
cleid=2372&category=384>

"**Snake reproduction**" Snaketype.com
<http://www.snaketype.com/snake-reproduction>

"The Care of California Kingsnakes / King Snakes"
ReptileKnowledge.com
<http://www.reptileknowledge.com/care/california-
kingsnake.php#ixzz4ZNEApJXs>
"Feeding Your Snake" PetSmart
<http://pets.petsmart.com/guides/snakes/feeding.shtml>

"Finding a reputable snake breeder online" PetSnakes.com
<http://pet-snakes.com/finding-reputable-snake-breeder-
online>

"Glossary" The Reptilian.co.uk
<http://www.thereptilian.co.uk/the_reptilian_glossary.html>

"Habitats: Cleaning and Disinfecting Reptile Cages"
PetEducation.com
<http://www.peteducation.com/article.cfm?c=17+1796&aid
=2847>

"How to Bathe a Snake" PetSnakes.com
<http://pet-snakes.com/bathe-snake>

"How to Clean a Snake Cage Quickly and Easily"
Reptile Knowledge
  <http://www.reptileknowledge.com/news/how-to-clean-a-
  snake-cage-quickly-and-easily/>

"Looking for a Pet Reptile? Consider a Breeder"
Erik J. Martin
<http://www.reptilesmagazine.com/Looking-for-a-Pet-
  Reptile-Consider-a-Breeder/>

"Pet Snakes for Sale – What to Do *Before* You Buy"
Brandon Cornett
  <http://www.reptileknowledge.com/care/pet-snakes.php>

"Reptile Tank Heating and Lighting Guide" Instructables
  <http://www.instructables.com/id/Reptile-tank-heating-
  and-lighting-guide/?ALLSTEPS>

"Snake Care Guide" LoveThatPet
<https://www.lovethatpet.com/small-pets/snakes/>

"Snake Habitats, How to Create" DrsFosterSmith.com
<http://www.drsfostersmith.com/PIC/Article.cfm?d=157&category=630&articleid=2383>

"Summary of State Laws Relating to Private Possession of Exotic Animals" Born Free USA
<http://www.bornfreeusa.org/b4a2_exotic_animals_summary.php>

Feeding Baby
Cynthia Cherry
978-1941070000

Axolotl
Lolly Brown
978-0989658430

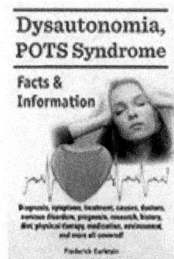

Dysautonomia, POTS
Syndrome
Frederick Earlstein
978-0989658485

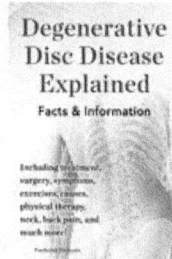

Degenerative Disc
Disease Explained
Frederick Earlstein
978-0989658485

Sinusitis, Hay Fever,
Allergic Rhinitis Explained
Frederick Earlstein
978-1941070024

Wicca
Riley Star
978-1941070130

Zombie Apocalypse
Rex Cutty
978-1941070154

Capybara
Lolly Brown
978-1941070062

Eels As Pets
Lolly Brown
978-1941070167

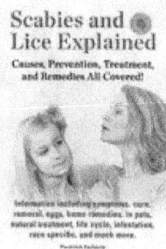

Scabies and Lice Explained
Frederick Earlstein
978-1941070017

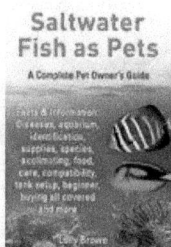

Saltwater Fish As Pets
Lolly Brown
978-0989658461

Torticollis Explained
Frederick Earlstein
978-1941070055

Kennel Cough
Lolly Brown
978-0989658409

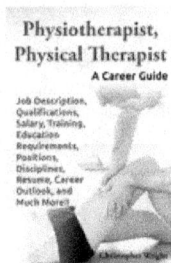

Physiotherapist, Physical
Therapist
Christopher Wright
978-0989658492

Rats, Mice, and Dormice
As Pets
Lolly Brown
978-1941070079

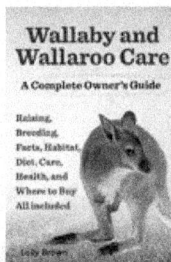

Wallaby and Wallaroo Care
Lolly Brown
978-1941070031

Bodybuilding Supplements
Explained
Jon Shelton
978-1941070239

Demonology
Riley Star
978-19401070314

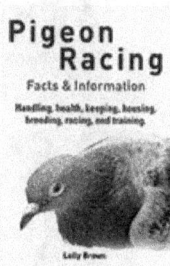

Pigeon Racing
Lolly Brown
978-1941070307

Dwarf Hamster
Lolly Brown
978-1941070390

Cryptozoology
Rex Cutty
978-1941070406

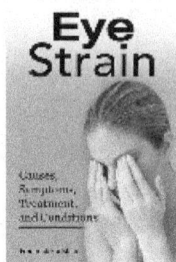

Eye Strain
Frederick Earlstein
978-1941070369

Inez The Miniature Elephant
Asher Ray
978-1941070353

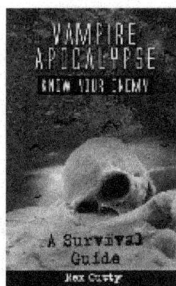

Vampire Apocalypse
Rex Cutty
978-1941070321